KELSO HIGH SCHOOL LIBRARY
KELSO, WASHINGTON

P9-ELT-949

X SCIENCE

AN IMAGINATION LIBRARY SERIES

by Jacqueline Laks Gorman

KELSO HIGH SCHOOL LIBRARY
KELSO, WASHINGTON

001.960R
06-290

Gareth Stevens Publishing
A WORLD ALMANAC EDUCATION GROUP COMPANY

Please visit our web site at: www.garethstevens.com
For a free color catalog describing Gareth Stevens Publishing's
list of high-quality books and multimedia programs,
call 1-800-542-2595 (USA) or 1-800-387-3178 (Canada).
Gareth Stevens Publishing's fax: (414) 332-3567.

Library of Congress Cataloging-in-Publication Data

Gorman, Jacqueline Laks, 1955-
    UFOs / by Jacqueline Laks Gorman.
        p. cm. — (X science: an imagination library series)
    Includes bibliographical references and index.
    Contents: Are we alone? — What are UFOs? — Recent UFO sightings —
What happened in Roswell? — Government secrets — Identified flying objects —
Fake UFO sightings — Reporting a UFO sighting — Serious searching.
    ISBN 0-8368-3201-9 (lib. bdg.)
    1. Unidentified flying objects—Juvenile literature. [1. Unidentified flying objects.]
I. Title. II. Series.
TL789.2.G67 2002
001.942—dc21   2002022511

Updated and reprinted in 2005.
First published in 2002 by
Gareth Stevens Publishing
A World Almanac Education Group Company
330 West Olive Street, Suite 100
Milwaukee, WI 53212 USA

Text: Jacqueline Laks Gorman
Cover design and page layout: Tammy Gruenewald
Series editor: Betsy Rasmussen
Picture Researcher: Diane Laska-Swanke

Photo credits: Cover © Mary Evans Picture Library; p. 5 NASA; pp. 7, 9, 11, 15, 17, 21
© Fortean Picture Library; p. 13 © Joel Sartore/NGS Image Collection; p. 19 Photofest

This edition © 2002 by Gareth Stevens, Inc. All rights reserved to Gareth Stevens, Inc. No part of
this book may be reproduced, stored in a retrieval system, or transmitted in any form or by any means,
electronic, mechanical, photocopying, recording, or otherwise without the prior written permission of
the publisher except for the inclusion of brief quotations in an acknowledged review.

Printed in the United States of America

3 4 5 6 7 8 9 09 08 07 06 05

Front cover: Mr. and Mrs. Paul Trent photographed
this UFO outside their house in McMinnville,
Oregon, in May 1950. It has never been explained.

TABLE OF CONTENTS

Words that appear in the glossary are printed in **boldface**
type the first time they occur in the text.

ARE WE ALONE?

What is in space besides the Sun, moons, stars, and planets? Could there be life on other planets? Could **aliens** be flying spaceships around?

Many people say that spaceships are out there, and some believe that aliens have visited our world.

Astronauts have seen strange things while they were in space. In May 1963, Gordon Cooper saw a glowing green object coming near his space capsule. In June 1965, Ed White and James McDivitt saw a weird metal object in space. In December 1965, James Lovell and Frank Borman saw something flying near their ship. These strange **sightings** have never been explained.

During the Apollo 11 mission to the Moon in July 1969, Neil Armstrong and Edwin "Buzz" Aldrin took this picture of a huge light near Earth. They also said they saw two UFOs on the Moon after they landed.

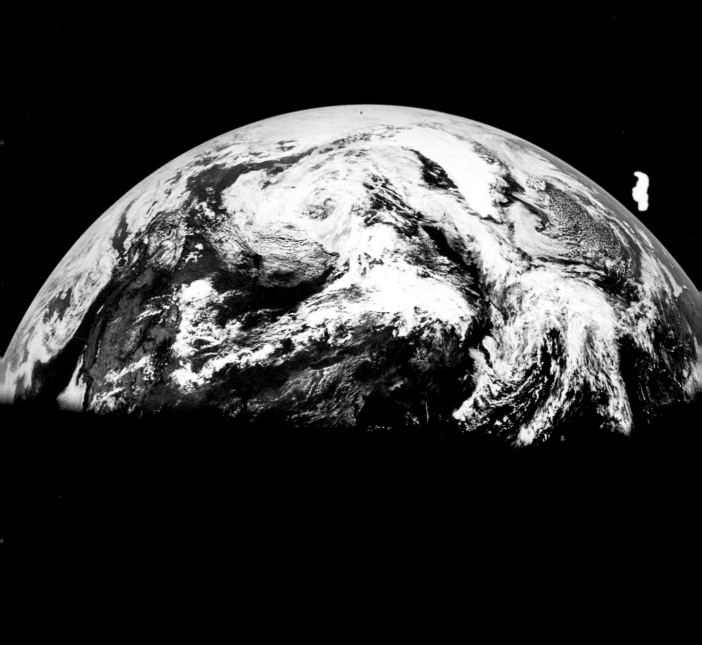

WHAT ARE UFOs?

UFOs are unidentified flying objects. These are objects that are seen by people, usually at night, that cannot be explained. Sometimes the objects look like disks, eggs, or cigars. Some of these objects glow and have lights. Some spin, hang in the sky, make sharp turns, or fly fast.

What are these strange objects? They could be **meteors**, weather balloons, or birds. They could be objects that people have imagined seeing. Or they could be alien spaceships.

Whatever these unexplained objects are, people have reported seeing them for thousands of years.

People in Basel, Switzerland, saw black globes floating over the city in 1566. Many stories of strange things in the sky exist all over the world and go back thousands of years.

RECENT UFO SIGHTINGS

The recent wave of UFO sightings began in 1947. A man named Kenneth Arnold was flying a small plane in Washington state. He saw nine silver objects flying together very fast. He said they looked like flying saucers.

In 1948, air force planes investigated a UFO sighting in Kentucky. A pilot had seen a huge metal object climbing high in the sky. He chased after it and crashed his plane.

Strange lights were seen over Washington, DC, for ten nights in 1952. The lights showed up on **radar** screens, and air force planes chased them. The lights came and went, slowed down and speeded up, and then disappeared.

Forty-eight people on a Brazilian ship saw this UFO over Trinidad in January 1958. It was shaped like the planet Saturn and flew in different directions at high speeds.

WHAT HAPPENED IN ROSWELL?

In 1947, something crashed near Roswell, New Mexico. A rancher found foil, metal, rubber, and other things on his land. The rancher told the sheriff about the rubble, and the sheriff told the nearby army base. First the army said a flying disk had crashed. Later, the army said it was a weather balloon that had crashed.

Not everyone believed this story, and some believed a spaceship had crashed. Some people even said they had seen dead aliens at the crash site. They said the government did an **autopsy** on one of the aliens.

In 1994, the air force admitted that what crashed was a secret government spy balloon.

Army Major Jesse Marcel looks at some of the things left behind by whatever crashed near Roswell. Many people still believe there is a government **conspiracy** to hide the truth and that aliens really landed in Roswell.

GOVERNMENT SECRETS

Is there a government plot to hide the truth about aliens? Some people think so. These people think the government has hidden spaceships and the bodies of aliens at air force bases in Nevada and Ohio.

The government did research on UFOs for about twenty years, beginning in the late 1940s. The researchers looked at thousands of cases of reported UFOs. They decided that most of the cases could be explained and were not alien spaceships.

The government may have good reasons not to tell the whole truth about UFOs. Sometimes the unexplained things people have seen were not spaceships but top-secret military planes.

The B-2 **Stealth** bomber was sometimes mistaken for a spaceship before it made its first official flight in 1989. It has a strange shape and flies silently high up in the sky.

IDENTIFIED FLYING OBJECTS

When a UFO sighting is explained, it becomes an "identified flying object." Many natural objects can be mistaken for spaceships. **Comets**, meteors, clouds, **ball lightning**, and distant tornadoes could be mistaken for UFOs. During the day, Venus can look very bright in the sky. Other planets, the Moon, and the star Sirius are often mistaken for spaceships. Even sunlight reflecting off flocks of birds can be confusing.

Things made by people can also be mistaken for spaceships. **Experimental** military planes, weather balloons, blimps, landing lights on planes, and even kites could all be mistaken for UFOs.

It is easy to see why someone might think this lenticular cloud is a spaceship. Lenticular clouds get their name from their smooth lens shape.

FAKE UFO SIGHTINGS

People have faked seeing UFOs many times. In the 1950s, a man named George Adamski said that he saw a spaceship land in California. Adamski said he got a ride in the ship with a man from Venus. Adamski wrote popular books about his adventure. It turned out that the spaceships in his pictures were all fakes, made of chicken feeders and bottles.

Two brothers named Dan and Grant Jaroslaw showed a picture they took of a UFO in 1967. Everyone thought it was a real spaceship. Nine years later, though, they admitted it was a model made from a Frisbee.

An airline pilot said he took this picture of a UFO in 1963. Years later, the UFO was shown to be a button. Hubcaps and models have also been used to fake photos of UFOs.

REPORTING A UFO SIGHTING

UFOs have been reported all over the world, but some places seem to be "hot spots" — places where UFOs are seen the most. More reports of UFO sightings come from Brazil than anywhere else in the world. The United States, Argentina, and parts of Europe are other hot spots.

In the United States, most reports of UFOs come from the Northeast and the Southwest. Most of these reports come from small towns and places near military bases.

UFO sightings are reported all the time. Groups around the world ask people to report any sightings they see. These groups then investigate the reports.

A glowing UFO comes down in front of some surprised witnesses. This picture is from the popular movie *Close Encounters of the Third Kind* (1977), about the landing of a spaceship.

SERIOUS SEARCHING

Are aliens visiting us? Scientists are looking for signs of **extraterrestrial** life. Researchers at the SETI (Search for Extraterrestrial Intelligence) Institute in California have been testing for radio signals from space for years. These researchers do not think that aliens have visited Earth, because they say that the nearest star is too far away for visitors to make the trip.

Other scientists, however, are looking for evidence of visiting alien ships. Project Hessdalen was set up in 1983 in Norway, where there are many UFO sightings. Cameras have been set up there. The cameras automatically record any strange lights in the sky.

Project Hessdalen in Norway has been active for years. This researcher checks a camera. It will record anything strange in the sky.

MORE TO READ AND VIEW

Books (Nonfiction)   *ETs and UFOs: Are They Real?* Larry Kettelkamp (Morrow Junior Books)

Flying Saucers. Opposing Viewpoints (series). Don Nardo (Greenhaven Press)

The Mystery of UFOs. Judith Herbst (Atheneum Books for Young Readers)

UFO Files: Out of this World . . . but True? Sean Plottner (Disney Press)

UFOs. Mysteries of Science (series). Elaine Landau (Millbrook Press)

UFOs and Aliens. The Unexplained (series). Colin Wilson (DK Publishing)

Unidentified Flying Objects and Extraterrestrial Life. Secrets of Space (series). Carole Marsh (Twenty-First Century Books)

Books (Fiction)   *Aliens Don't Wear Braces. Adventures of the Bailey School Kids* (series). Debbie Dadey and Marcia Thornton Jones (Little Apple)

Bruce Coville's Book of Aliens II: More Tales to Warp Your Mind. Bruce Coville, editor (Apple)

I Was a Sixth Grade Alien. I Was a Sixth Grade Alien (series). Bruce Coville (Aladdin Paperback)

Martians Don't Take Temperatures. Adventures of the Bailey School Kids (series). Debbie Dadey and Marcia Thornton Jones (Little Apple)

Videos (Nonfiction)   *Kidnapped by UFOs?* (WGBH Boston Video)

Secrets of the Unknown: UFOs. (MPI Home Video)

The Unexplained: Alien Abductions. (A&E)

Videos (Fiction)   *Close Encounters of the Third Kind.* (Columbia/Tristar Studios)

It Came from Outer Space. (Universal Studios)

22

WEB SITES

Web sites change frequently, but we believe the following web sites are going to last. You can also use good search engines, such as **Yahooligans!** [www.yahooligans.com] or **Google** [www.google.com] to find more information about UFOs. Some keywords that will help you are: *UFOs, extraterrestrials, Roswell, aliens,* and *flying objects.*

www.ajkids.com

Ask Jeeves Kids, the junior Ask Jeeves site, is a great place to do research. Try asking:
> What are UFOs?
> Are UFOs real?
> Have aliens landed on earth?

You can also just type in words and phrases with "?" at the end, such as:
> Extraterrestrials?
> Flying saucers?

www.yahooligans.com

This junior version of the Yahoo site is very easy to use. Simply type in the letters "UFO" to get a list of sites appropriate for kids.

www.cufos.org

This site of the *Center for UFO Studies*, an international group that scientifically investigates UFOs, has everything you want to know about UFOs — history, photos, reports, and more.

www.iufomrc.com

This fun site is from the *International UFO Museum and Research Center* in Roswell, N.M. Here you will find plenty of material on the Roswell incident, museum exhibits, a newsletter, and even a Kids' Club.

www.hessdalen.org

Learn all about *Project Hessdalen*, an ongoing scientific study in Norway where there have been lots of UFO sightings.

www.seti.org

The *SETI* Institute is dedicated to searching for signs of intelligent life in space. Its web site discusses the possibility of the existence of other life forms in the universe.

www.pbs.org/wgbh/nova/aliens

This companion site for the *NOVA* television show shares stories about people who believe in alien abductions and those who do not.

GLOSSARY

You can find these words on the pages listed. Reading a word in a sentence helps you understand it even better.

aliens (AY-lee-uhns) — beings from another planet. 4, 6, 10, 12, 20

astronauts (AS-truh-nawtz) — people who travel in space. 4

autopsy (AW-top-see) — the examination of a body after death. 10

ball lightning (BAWL LYT-neen) — a rare type of lightning in which lighted balls float in the air. 14

comets (KAHM-ehts) — in space, bright bodies with a fuzzy head and a long tail. 14

conspiracy (kuhn-SPIHR-uh-see) — to secretly do something wrong. 10

experimental (eks-peer-eh-MEHN-tehl) — trying out a new idea, activity, or procedure. 14

extraterrestrial (EKS-truh-tuh-REHS-tree-uhl) — involving outer space. 20

meteors (MEE-tee-urrz) — pieces of rock or metal, from space, that burn when they enter the Earth's atmosphere. 6, 14

radar (RAY-dahr) — a machine that bounces radio waves off objects to find them. 8

sightings (SYT-eens) — things that have been seen. 4, 8, 16, 18

stealth (STELTH) — acting secretly and quietly. 12

INDEX